D0070990

Exorcism Lessons in the Heartland

Cara Dees

Exorcism Lessons in the Heartland

Cara Dees

Barrow Street Press
New York City

©2019 by Cara Dees
All rights reserved

Cover Art: *The Birds* by Anne Siems
Art Direction by Laura Marciano
Designed by Michelle Caraccia

Published 2019 by Barrow Street, Inc.
(501) (c) 3) corporation. All contributions are tax deductible.
Distributed by:
    Barrow Street Books
    P.O. Box 1558
    Kingston, RI 02881

Barrow Street Books are also distributed by Small Press Distribution,
SPD, 1341 Seventh Street Berkeley, CA 94710-1409, spd@spdbooks.org;
(510) 524-1668, (800) 869-7553 (Toll-free within the US); amazon.com;
Ingram Periodicals Inc., 1240 Heil Quaker Blvd, PO Box 7000,
La Vergne, TN 37086-700 (615) 213-3574; and Armadillo & Co., 7310
S. La Cienega Blvd, Inglewood, CA 90302, (310) 693-6061.

Special thanks to the University of Rhode Island English Department and
especially the PhD Program in English, 60 Upper College Road, Swan
114, Kingston, RI 02881, (401) 874-5931, which provides valuable
in-kind support, including graduate and undergraduate interns.

First Edition

Library of Congress Control Number: 2019944371

ISBN 978-0-9973184-9-4

for my mother, who made existence home

CONTENTS

Epode

Most open shape, I can't measure out
        the silver fragments

of your loosed sea – I keep haloing
        back to your thin walk

to our shed, when winter stuttered
        for a week, and the sun

widened warm, and the pasture's cold
        poverty lifted to breath,

and you eased ice-torn feet over the stones
        to the stallion that shared

your fierce weakness for clemency –
        when you held out

your palm to his teeth, and the light grew
        wild over your hand.

I

Vigil

Before the Diagnosis, Spring

Now the nestlings' hunger cry
is an anguish shaped

for your ears alone, and the trembling
of hickory another voice

that descends, out of temper
from the too long winter,

to you. For you, flushed guardian
of the spring garden,

all that calls calls full-throated.
Nothing is still,

not the refrain the leaves smooth
mild over the dawn,

not the sun's dizzying throat.
Even the brace of ponies

devouring the field mouths
the armor from your heart.

In its silence their words blow open,
Hear us. For you – we.

Their tails shake like the sky.
It is too much

and it is not enough,
the wealth of you

stretching endlessly, far wheat to far
wheat. And it isn't that

your quick wrists quicken the wind
in its turn or that the soil

self-sculpts to your palm,
but as if living things

spirited their sadnesses to you,
dead center in you,

who looms so small and strange in them.
A total apartness absorbing

blue field, blue atmosphere, and,
from an urban elsewhere,

your father's slow starvation –
he whom one by one

the nurses forget, who drifts
up and down corridors

to awaken his thinned legs,
his cheekbones far

too far apart . . . The white film
that bubbles in the corners

of his mouth winds your dreams
tight as winter.

And your last words to me
please help me when

three years later you fight to rise
from the bed for the toilet,

maybe even now they are with you,
a diminutive ill ringing.

As with every spring, I watch you
from my bedroom where

I compose my histories and I dream
of containing you in me,

of being a new blue grove
you could echo in.

Your words, my words. Then
it would be easy for you

to forget the names you call yourself,
the uncountable names

that others narrow against you,
to sing *under the green-*

sweet canopy I dreamed of love
and love found me

upward, upward. But spring
urges on too many forms,

like the earth voicing the bulbs cutting
it loose, beaks claiming

the fluid bodies exposed there. Aflame,
you lift your face

to the surface of the sun. It breeds
a cruel harvest within.

Vigil for Another Onset

I write: when you heard the news,
you secured the windows. The glass

expanded, azured against the pine,

half-sealed our exits. One by one,
north-facing walls buckled.

Preferred words canceled

their footprints. No *persimmon*
could survive within that sirenpeal, no

strike aflame. Wrong to write, perhaps,

but true: in that place, your cancer
was the steadiest presence.

Bluing, mute, we toured the storm,

heaved steaming water to the mares,
disquieted the stunned apple branches.

We lingered in the furious anti-ink,

bending with it or against it, whichever
motion curbed best the cold, considered

the vague symmetry stiffening

the clinquant oak, the wild hare.
When the storm magnified and teethed,

breaking us open rib by rib

and rummaging every heartplace
of us, it lodged itself inside.

We housed it, kept it, stitching

around it our wounded torsos.
Wrong to do, perhaps, but true.

We carried it with us: the news,

the glass, the footprint, the apple,
the ink, the frozen weight.

The Mound

(Your body weakening, I change the bed around you.)

The largeness of it
stayed me. I had forgotten
how the rise and slope is not

nothing, how we have shape,
an oval that is real, and real,
undying, headlong moss.

I looked away when you did.
The mound rose and fell
and did not think of blushing.

In your steady, antiseptic
panic, you could not have been
more naked, more at mercy –

you, with the windswept face,
the shameless biceps!
So I switched the red

cotton sheets for the new beige
silk feast; I tucked away
your silvering curve.

Those last weeks, you did not speak
of your god who spoke only
of a longer summer.

His was a hugeness turned
anatomical. Spent and wordless,
you refused to humor him.

I fell to smoothing over you
the threads' dry shelter.
We kept our own company.

Three Exposures

Versailles on a white morning

Beneath cherubic
skyscape, carved and mirrored gilt,

breathless limestone, all

that wakeful glory
of *le mort saisit le vif,*

your feet swell and ache

again, your liver
darkly dappled, another

bout of chemo gone

awry. South of us,
langue d'oc collapses

indefinitely.

Wisconsin in summer

If you were clear of
this oversun and -hurt, the

light would mourn your shape.

Wisconsin in winter

Awake a moment
you spot a fox, a single

glimmer in the snow,

and we remaining
can't find it. Hay slants empty

to iced ground. Then your

sudden vigilance
outblooms and you drop, somnam-

bulistic, into

the wheelchair you hate,
drifting past the glazed walls, not

seeing me see you.

Vigil Series Closing with Hyacinths

Returning to Your Childhood Bedroom, New Year's Eve

December closes but you're still dreaming
of its undone globe, of countless days stretching
and opening above you. The clock stiffens,
signing its name against your eyelids. Fire

bristles the lake. Rooms away, your daughters
gaze awake. Their bodies, rich with hours,
age recklessly. Their long hair grows longer.
What's winter to you, timestamped? What's winter

to the housewife in flames? A heap of cream.
A rind scoring itself to pith. Chemo
run another round. So instead you dream
of your own hours melting, kind to kind,

into the silver, as the fireworks tilt
hungrily toward you, as you wed the snow.

You Have Two to Three Months, Maybe Less

In spring they   cull you, the doctors, those dreams
        of a beyond-   territory, built with

clean human minds   in concord, chimed
        to a single knell; shrines   astonished with

burnt sacrifice stacked   under a cut-white
        sun. To eat, eating, will be   eaten. To

make of misfortune   a cleansing, a mild
        matité, a morning   rising and rose-

trimmed. In winter they   reassemble you
        (the battered veins, the   glitching beat) among

their likenesses, with   smudged armor,   thumbscrew
        CT scans, those whose   gazes ferry them

from yours taking them in, who   won't say they
        sold you anything   like wonder or hope.

Waiting

> *She'd given you an impossible task:*
> *she said to follow and you intended to.*
> — Brenda Hillman, "First Tractate"

Halfway up the steps the blood's clamor stands
silenced. We slant down, my arm between you
and the stripped pine that would rise to you.
I need to rest. Fingers gray on the washed

knots, you balance. The night, directionless,
sways and balances. Between the queen bed
(of metal, of feather) you can't climb to
and the hospital bed (plastic on pine)

you refuse to occupy, stairs occur
endlessly. Here is the sick hook, the catch
in the breath between wanting and struck need —
waiting weak-armed, ashamed, for my father

to brook the solid cold back to our house
and hoist you upward, to a crawl again.

After Waiting

Then your crawling stopped and the rooms gave up
their corners. We were not prepared for words

to heap edgelessly, for frames astonished
by glass. *We* went wrong; without you it slipped

slantwise, formed new mouths. For weeks hyacinths
burned accents on the sills, brash-heart contra-

dictions that unnerved us almost as much
as the rhonchus that had seethed from your chest.

December locked down but January
would not close. Will not. It sounds its half-globe

above our house as a current without
calm skims a lowland with no growing thing.

But dreams of the thinnest umbrage of you
still dazzle. Raw haze, they coax. They kidnap.

Hymeneal

I dreamed you living again –

clear, slim as a slip
of birch in strong wind,

nineteen-year-old girl-woman
who would speak but lacked
a tongue. The church many-

windowed, the sun lifting
its white hair over the congregation's

closed face. They waited
for your wild lord to enter, he
whose new ring your finger

belonged to. They waited
for you to speak, your slim

wick-voice, yet your every limb
burning a tender perimeter,
a sweet marginalia. I rose

to speak for you, to unlock
our scattering from my throat,

the sun shaking its living
hair over my eyes. Guttural –
there was no small place

my cry could take hold in.
The crowd chittered, grinned.

You stood quiet and undone
as you waited for the lover
with eyes smooth as stone

to rise stark before you, for
the long day to stave in below you.

Thorn Creek, Summer

I tell you I want a different life,
like yours but without the sorrow.

Then your voice – high, surprised
in the climbing provender:

I like my life. I like my life.

Eclogue

i. You say you always planned on dying on the deck in the
summer, surrounded by flowers

As if thought could make it so, could swell
your light, domesticate and expel a hounding dark,

all seasons become one green, to-be-opened
asylum. Look. There are no watchtowers

unbarring their warmth to your lessening breath.
No heavy sun arranges itself for you –

it wills its head down to whitening meadow.
Already the smooth good-byes you arranged

in your mind for years are undeliverable.
They hollowed when you did. Look, now.

This land is dazed. It is vast and without sound.

ii. You say I'm the one who'll have to live with it

Live with – what? The cracked iris garden.
The timothy fields, rigid with winter, dwarfed

with debt. Your herds of dreamy, opaque horses.
No, those I love like my own chapel. *It* is not

field or garden or horse. And you – you will
un-live with – what? You who will pierce new

and desolate arteries unlike any summer bird
diving the water. You who will grow expert

in soliloquy, its falling tides and sheer poverty.
It is not our danger. It is only the after-storm,

the river already stolen from the shore.

iii. You say you wanted to see what I would be like when I was thirty

Strange, the hour bitten off, or clipped like
caged fowl. How things of basic fortune

unpin from us: the bronzed sage resown,
my voice large and gentle with age, your hair

at last shouldering its genuine white. Remember
when you bloomed thirty, alone on ruined

farmland, and not-alone also, a small human
crescent waxing speech inside you.

If my middle self, stolen from the center
of my life, met you then, our faces

would enter one another – a mirror's offering,
origin and replica, signature and plagiarist.

We would mingle and divorce like those
spires of dry sage, their ardency,

my every sigh seamless with your sigh.

iv. You say you can't wake up

as you face me with eyes beyond memory.
A wilderness whistles among blue grooves,

blanching the hickory of its doves.
Bare as a needle, you thin to ellipsis.

Don't leave, please. You're my last witness.

Weight

i

It was when you lifted me, muted

and blued, the marble fixed
in my throat, its hard cat's eye
larger than all the gathering plea

of my six years of breath, when
your field-reddened arms pumped

the voice back out of my ghosting torso,
that it came home – how closely
my air studied your maze of nerves,

traced and recited the wires
of your muscle. And after, when

the blackout waxed across my eyes
and ushered bright words into the feral dark,
how your weight held, cleared me.

ii

And when, years later, among

cresting snow and bleached
oak, you mouthed aimlessly,
your tongue fibrous and gritted,

and I pressed the carnation-pink
Toothette over the thrush stretching

toward your tonsils, that I glimpsed
how unaccompanied was the ache
within my pulse, how entirely your mind

set off on its solitary exile.
And when you could talk, you talked

of a living delirium – of my sister's face
become a rash of meat, and the ceiling
voided to shadow, and ice-white

July weddings without anything
that coarsens, that withers – until

you coughed black blood and, your trachea
strewn with sap, we detached the misted
cannula. Then I felt it – the cut anchor, how

you weighted my selfish, singing life.

II

Fragments of the Afteryears

Halfway through the Book I'm Writing

after Lynn Emanuel

My mother's hand   the wildwanderer
reaches for mine   I

look and her hand is not   there suddenly

my words are larger   than the dirty
teeth & plead of poetry   *Stop writing* she says

she does not say stop writing   *Who wants to read*

of dead horses dead   chunks of sky dead
me? Give me living wheat   mornings bluely entering

give me the vast   atrium of christian kindness

Such poems I say are neon   spilling over
shining real mess into   warm ether

Perhaps bright life too is real   She does not say

stop writing   *Stop writing* she says
Cities away from her   murmuring ashes

the catalpa tree is flush   with the smell of semen

with mockingbirds   I say tell me
what to write   she says   *stop*

write   stop   write   stop   write

Vigil Hemming In

Lightless light and my father's cigarette

smoke softening into it and the light
complicit with the smoke and softening, too,

into the field's hitherto horizon, the field

a blur of turned drumlin. A flick of ash
and a mottled dove melts into the failing hickory.

So this is the sunset with you removed –

a circle withdrawing into a deeper circumference,
and so on. Then some. When you were,

light knew its home and kept within it.

Names held their course. Each poem chose
one headstrong color and became it utterly,

not like this blownback space, this all-

over sound, where *petal* can mean *mare pressed
to ground*, can mean *little girl lost, little woman

stormbound*. Words need edges to survive. Or else,

this hickory and its gathering of doves, this everywhere-
song, this widower burning behind the window.

Complicated Grief

Between his wife's missing and the killing
        of the injured horse, he moved through dooms
                and, dooming, learned to keep
the windthrown house she had kept
        for him. Between the killing of the injured horse
                and the killing of the horse gone blind
he streamlined her closet, discarding
        the shapeless jeans, the ruined
                sateen bras. Before any horse
flayed her hoof like a shucked oyster,
        before any blind horse stumbled into
                her mother's quicksilver kick, before any
of that other bigger missing, he repeated
        to his daughters, *Never be a vet.*
                They repeated it back, both parents
in their particular darknesses no more than
        the cotton muddied against their knees,
                their backs. And they said it again, later,
his wife become no more than wayward ether
        rummaging their skulls, *never,* as he urged
                his feet into boots stiff with manure
and blood to deliver another womb-
        dead calf, *never, I promise,* learning
                the care his creatures demanded him.

Windfall

My father resuscitates a paralyzed woman, Independence Day

You find her in summer's stubble
of alfalfa, facedown, a scratch

in the dirt. Reliably, horizontally, her road
repeats itself into the heat waves

that drag it out to frailness. Her face
turned to the furrows. Her breath

another climate, an open, clastic space
with countless doors and with no doors.

A pulse's faint burn, a chink in the
hatchway, and the breath

comes through to you in sobs. Still,
too much blue spills into her eyes,

as though an unlived land scraped

its hills against them, her spine left
piecemeal to the steady dark.

No knowing now, how her entrances
will take shape, what becomes

of her side-roads, her private paths. The soul
unravels, re-spins as it will: a native

hazard, a windfall. The ambulance gone,
you stand alone again in the hay.

Your doctor's hands, pickpockets
of those unlit lands, again alone.

Lying Old Together

Their limbs contain familiar weather.
Their breathing tapers to slow frost.

The cold domes of his lungs flutter.
Almost carelessly, she casts a feather-

tendoned arm over his meagerness.
Their hearts fasten, one in the other.

Theirs is the thinnest living harmony.
Darling, we will never come close.

Tending

She stops to shout out to me that she was my mother
I'm obliged to believe her because of the nettle
— Vénus Khoury-Ghata, "Orties,"
translated by Marilyn Hacker

And yet their bright nerves
                    nudge up beyond the clay again

and they gulp the sun into
                    their fruiting. The quiet-

living mound of lenten roses:
                    sting and downheartedness.

Summers ago we worked
                    together, syllableless,

thorns breaching our palms,
                    the truncated stalks heaped and

gathering weight at the garden's edge,
                    shaping a thing ready to be burnt.

The ghost moth larvae already
                    at work against the missing root.

Today's summer, the stems' threads
                    open again against

my shears, I think how
                    what I've tended to is shunted

into a fiercer atmosphere, how
                    it wilds, onely, with its needle.

After Arriving Home from Church and Learning Our Dogs Were Shot, Their Bodies in the Fields

For weeks I walked the shoulderless road,
calling.   *Welcome,*
the wind psalmed back, *your feed*

is wanting teeth. The swamp
sighed odes   to silence, concerned
with its bounty of skunk,

its possum. I called to my mild
black dog with   delicate eyes,
to my timid golden dog missing

a leg, to the modest calm
of our house,   driven out
entire, to the hollow silage.

I walked and called. I thought,
voices get tired, too,   they run away
with the body, and the body

mislays so easily its claw and howl.
Like how,   twenty years later,   I watch
you – your blunt silence

among the summering of the hymnals,
driven out   of yourself
on the velvet interior, calling me.

What Mercy

Together, we   drove them to panic.
          Saliva soaped   their fine mouths
their precise chests.   What is the horse except
          a softer autumn   the human except

a luckier set of teeth?   Mother unsung
          & elsewhere   whose hand first
curled your churchgirl   hand to a fist?
          When the neighbors   licensed in injury

stalked the almond-   tipped & shatterable
          does of our forest   what reckless mercy
sent you unarmed   to chase the men out
          your own kind-eyed   ponies trussed

& bitted?   Here (my half-
          life) now   (without) defend the day
you taught me   to whip mares   to force-wean
          foals.   They were more

innocent   than we gave them credit for
          (hurt earth, hot-   & hurt-hearted).
Mother undone   their kindness was
          they could not   speak against us.

Reservoirs

of leather, of pulsing almond, and eyes
like soft storms falling in swaled meadows.
Our oldest stumbles into her fifth cycle
and a life-urge oozes from her with the pap,

a pinched yield for the likes of which
her owners will ruin her. Beyond her swamp
of shit and stale blood, hutches stream
white on white. Inside, still soiled

from the heat of the womb, the nameless
calves waver on skinny legs and yell.
Their mother is straw, formula, slap, kick.
They expect nothing from us, and less.

Piccinini's "The Long Awaited"

after Marianne Moore's "The Fish"

Her
frame's utter
    ruin, the unsolvable magic
    that roams her, that folds sick
        skin to water, the missed tension

a
nebula
    of sweetness, sweetness caught up in the
    body's dazed proof – she dreams
        upon the son, as the smell of

torn
lace would warm
    the sudden air. Free-form age, foreign
    pulse – these things tiptoe in.
        And the boy with the serious,

shut
smile, what
    easy rest drifts shadowless over
    him, patterns them torso
        to torso? How neatly does peace

limb
inside him,
    so that any rush of grief broadens
    and falls to softer ground?
        The sea grows heavier in them.

My
minus-sight,
      my viscera, smoke to my winter,
      their story is not our
            story. Your every violet scent

died
terrified,
      spindled to a deep sour you could not
      name. Your homespun chroma caught
            and cored to woad thread, turned cinder.

Too
grace-askew,
      heavenbent, see-through, that glassy pair.
      She, calmed billow; he, com-
            posed coil. Death is not their affair.

Exorcism Lessons in the Heartland

The spirit best enters the body
as sleep enters – as the body

inhabiting itself unseen. Here

is the chapel. Here is the audience
of promised children, a village

unequipped and force-fellowed.

They think the sun is a good
and strange hymn, a huge oneness

feasting on itself, a proud husband

to itself. They think their village
must be a necessary enemy. When

the preacher mimics the demoned

people they think they themselves
are demoned, the unseen are sick

for the housing of their bodies,

their mutual oneness. Their future
bodies must be made to possess

an uncommon discipline. When the spirit

enters they think of untouched water, of
a golden book closing over their names.

Abduction

after Nuala Ní Dhomhnaill's "Fuadach,"
translated by Michael Hartnett

The fairy woman lodges her foot
   in the door of the poem
and the hours after dark

edge in with her. If lucky,
   I will have composed
a thin-steamed meal for your

habitual place and she will calm
   and lock down to it, jawing
your wheat. If I'm unlucky,

she will let fall her contempt
   for my undaughterly kitchen,
claim the keys to your spirit

cellar and, lit with the freed
   wine you never opened,
she will erase your half-

realized ledgers, rend
   your remnant garments.
And still you watch her

from the night-coupled fields,
   caught in the diminishing
crawl space of her voice. *Crumbs*

before poems, the fairy woman says.
   Write her out, you answer
wordlessly. *Write her out of your house.*

III

After Tremor

Tanka After-Hours

i

As if we could mend
        together the dead's over-
lonely hours to one

        filament of ether, a
                blushing tongue of song, an edge.

ii

Once, in our highest
        versing, I wanted the claim
on my blood to be-

        night my body for hers, for
                hers to be lifted in turn.

iii

Is the dead mother
        a nothing to the daughter's
hybrid hours, or do

        the windows rise to her as
                a volume lengthens within?

iv

And after, the peace
            speaking closely with us, we
cannot contain it

            all. Shut transport and absence
                        now again a constant root.

Now I'm a foregone conclusion, the voices in my head talk and talk . . .

They say, no woman spent by man rights herself
aright (again). She fashions another pleadpiece for her
power-bitten heart and soon she is a witch at work
against the flora-ed mothers – good/dirt-kissed/
wage-begone – moving her best for their calamity.

The woman says, once there were two too many hands
against my principal surfaces. I was burgundied/
whipped with drink/shoeless/far from
myself, when his hands turned disciplined
over me. His body dug along/into/through/
beyond mine. I lost the residue of an inner summer.

They say, listen, O disaligned. The man is what
the woman folds into when her oneness betrays/over-
shares her (again). Her mouth closed is a shameful thing;
her mouth noising is a worse. A holed body is holiday
for a brotherhood, a kingdom for a stronger eating.

The woman says, the afterday I fixed him
espresso in bed and put my sense/guilt/grief to rest
for one absolute/unused year. Until, that is,
the stiff factory of marginalia started up
and all my windows freed to a dirty flare. Until
I woke again, overvexed/overworded/tired/grown old.

John Roberts,
following the Burwell v. Hobby Lobby decision

Because I will be fertilized at least once
            before a calmer weather mounts against me
                        (as a loosened fault governs the tipped cup),

I dedicate to your softest glancing-aways
            the zeroes of me, my gush and heft
                  as ready kindling. All I ask

is an orderly sacrifice, to be a pool that trills
            according to the flatness of your palm.
                     How could I know unless you told me

the scope of my indiscretions, how
            I cut down every one of the fences
                  to my pastures before I nursed them

into flame? My best tribute: one
            skein of callow wool, the faint sway
                  of a real wimple, and, stitched

with cattail and new junegrass,
            a turtledove's close nest. You will like it, John,
                  the sun already painting the thin center

a free and fire-steady purple.
            You will like how it blooms the light
                  inside it – absolutely, thoughtlessly – like

the eyes of good women. Even so
            my gifts are simple – scraps of weeds
                  and field detritus, common plumage.

John, I keep thinking – if instead I gave you
      my heart, culled from the hurt daughter
            of my body, if I lifted it from the ribs'

vital claw, would you have me
      as you want me? Then I could be
            a thing that is weighed in the hand

of a man, to be found ample
      or wanting, to be lifted to the startled
            mouth, to be swallowed in shock

or with admiration. Then I could be pink
      and bound against your tongue, adopted
            at last into you, your firmer borders.

To the Supreme Associate Judges,

. . . For we be, either of us, weary of other.
- Medbh McGuckian, "The Good Wife Taught Her Daughter"

Today the sun re-struck a path   along my neck and loosened
down my shoulder blades and as I reddened

beneath its poor man's kiss   I remembered how
I never sued for your forgiveness, viz.,
my hair's continuous shambling,   the flushed confusion

of my face, my purse
without a penny. Honor Tenor   or Uproar or Bitter, please

advise how to best mend
my pastures' bruised fences,   how much soap mixed
with how much spirit to sleek

the oiled curve of my frontispiece,   how little I must love
my windows. My words want

your honeyed distinction, the rigid-   lily of your voice,
so I can fetch only the crude truth
            for my writing you –   this morning the sun

fierced over and through me
            toward our ill-bred mare who, warmed

            and kicking, bit   her new colt's stomach
to patchwork. He stumbles alone, mouthing
            with lack of purpose.   The truth is I'm frightened

            of his obsession with her thick salary
of milk and it reminds me   how my mother would counsel me

against men, *hold, hold, hold*
            on, hold, and I held,   until I didn't.
And after I wanted to cry to her, *Look!*

There are no limits   to this well, no end
            to the body's stretched felicity! Forgive me,
Honor Melt or Hammer or   Temper. This body

can be a careless companion, bucking beyond me,
all heat and hormone,   headland and early

summer. Please reply with guidance as to:
item fence, freeing;   item sun, forwarding;

item body, slapdash rose. I wait here
for your letter, that law   you lay down – exact,
exacting – those words louder, larger than my own.

56

To the Next Supreme Justice,

There were also a few hundred looking into abortion through bleaching one's uterus . . .
– Seth Stephens-Davidowitz, The New York Times

Madam or most likelier   Sir, surely by now
    you have noticed   the smell of women, salt-dark
sulfur, flour, flower, sweat   lifting from downturned limbs

after long afternoons in the fields.   When I go milking
    it seems my smell   is everywhere & if

    my letters to your co-   elder-judges survive
I like to think   my bloodbreathing scent   has been driven out
of their pages until   almond, cream, clean   grass alone remain.
    Smooth & blank   as brochures.

    I tell myself I must be   a fresher midwest   I must be
cleaner than any harvest   a pasture swept of dust
all my beasts housed   elsewhere. I tell myself   one must allow oneself

to be kept, from time   to time one must accept being
         stripped down & stored.   Future Honor

the fact is I need counsel   how best to go on
correctly, to go on   with correct living, to go on   with living. e.g.,
         the film in which men   lock an iron clamp onto

            a cow's butterfly haunches   & hoist her bodily

from her rank bed of straw   for her morning milking.

e.g., the tumor on my mother's wrist   purpling, sharpening, until
         she smashed it with a dictionary   collapsed   from the blood-

               crush drumming into her   then rose & balanced

back over the gravel   to return to barn work.

When she settled into death   a penny-sized violet
         still swelled beyond   her yellowed wrist.
               Un-   faced, Un-   fazed,
bodies without governance   require close strategy.

58

If a mare overruns an electric fence   she must be wooed back
into the warmer calm.   Only after are the wires
restitched, the current   reswitched, her herd

held in place.   Last night I dreamed
of the road thinning into   a distance hidden beyond my father's farm
& all along it   snow, wire, current.   I await eagerly your response

the response of your brothers   in this our hour
of bleached throats, our year   two thousand sixteen.

Resurrected, a version of my mother dwells in silence

, surveys the pasture   in retrograde, the autumn-
       blasted grass, near the down fence

the heirloom tomatoes shrouded in fuzz,
       dwindling on threads.   As she remains

no friend to forced speech   or any forced rupture
       of stillness, she mirrors the budding

permafrost, the flattened stems.   That is to say,
       any words she sheltered have already

surrendered themselves   to homesickness.
       I speak so as to speak, selecting

calm and calming   topics: new hybridities
       of apple, my longer hair. For days

she has realmed the garden, accumulating
       mist and bone   as I dream her answering.

A poet once told me that dreams are boring
       and it's true, but   my want for her voice

drills my sleep. If she speaks of time,   then time. If money,
       money. I'm not picky. My mother loved

counting money, which she understood to be a transaction
       between beautiful and necessary things.

So I dream her counting silver //   one, two // heaping
       clear gold for faster surgeries   she couldn't buy.

, centers first her inner ashes, then
        tendons her middle, then   hardens, softens,

hardens. Since dying   I suspect she's acquired facts
        I stored from her and harbors

an altered view of our relationship, wonders
        why I did not tell her   what I did not tell her:

the ready alibi of gin and wine, the wilted dress,
        the refusal   he pushed against.

, palinodes my dreams. // I never said
        I wanted to die   surrounded by flowers.

Of course I lied. I knew what you
        would be like when you were thirty.

I never said   I couldn't wake up. //

. If she still loves me   in the style she lived in,
         true-blue and jealous, I can

take her pain for me for granted, like
         good health, but as I think this she drifts

above the fire we build for her in the garden,
         returns briefly   to ash, then glass,

her body fluent only with the dusk
         salting the hickory.   Years ago,

while driving to church, my father promised her
         he'd kill himself   after she died.

My sister and I   in the backseat, not speaking,
         our parents steadily blooming terror

before us.   We couldn't figure out
         how to un-hurt them. Tonight

the same caesura settles down again to write
         its chapters, publishing them   between us.

, listens   or does not listen
          to my sister and the liquid trilling

of her flute. The flute was a present
          from my mother and father,   with a gold mouthpiece

and wild roses carved   across the silver body.
          With it my sister be-angels the apple trees.

My mother responds   by not responding.
          Gnats empty the field and settle our arms.

There are kinds of emptiness I'm only now learning
          to recognize, coda   with no closing inside them.

A poet once told me   to speak explicitly
          about the night I was   rummaged through, that

without details a poem is incomplete,
          but most of what I remember   is not remembering.

On my stomach.   Pale yellow walls.
          Outside there must   have been trees.

Her breath and fingers by now automatic,
          my sister continues hoisting notes above us.

, flickers her edges like   a light trap, but mostly
        does nothing, the farmhouse

stubbornly occupying   the quiet beyond her.
        Her fire-rivered hands,   wringing,

workless.   When we were living, she
        always worked. The day after I was born

she circuited back to her place
        in my father's office, resumed her counting.

She said this overwork explained
        why I couldn't speak   until I was four, except

to twist vowels into a code   only my sister
        could decipher. My parents and I

rehearsed *r*'s and *s*'s over dinner until
        I recited the Lord's Prayer   effortlessly.

The week she died   my mother transcribed
        tight lists of numbers, penning

unintelligible notations. The floors of the caesura tilted,
        decoupled. Even money   trembled away from her.

, drops in on my dreaming and frowns
         at the poem.   // Okay, I say to her,

this is not the resurrection I would have
         chosen, although   I have chosen it.

The other one looks like this –   wealth of beach
         and gold-rush sunset. No need to speak. //

, holds vigil   over the page I give her,
        pen in hand. In a blaze

she could make or unmake   the poem, set a line
        to rights, strikethrough unkempt

ephemera. But if she dwells inside
        this blue ash of a door   of a soul, it means

she lies low in a cold room we can only reach
        through a high window.   I take the page

from her, turn it against the light.
        Hover it over the stove.   No strikethrough.

No message. A poet once told me not to write
        in the voices of the dead;   they won't correct you

if you get it wrong and you will   get it wrong.
        They are always only memory run wild.

That is to say, the dead have   no sides to them,
        no fixed container, like silence. Reader,

you know by now   as you knew before
        she does not visit the poem. Should

her mouth burst into   whole languages
        it will be inside another   unspeakable radius.

. I speak so as to speak: women are written either
                as pomegranates (once opened

the juice lacking   jurisdiction) or
                as human. Left alone, the mind will either

torch its own bridges or dovetail its own
                lovely grooves. What kind of silence

is a blown coil, what kind   a correct gift
                floating the ill current. Days before my mother died

my sister read to her from a book
                in which young girls cut their hair for money.

I read her the only poem   she heard me read.
                We were trying. We   were trying to build windows

through to her, over the body's   softening architecture, into
                the smudge of mist she worked inside, counting.

After Tremor

For years my body remembered
        before I did and shut up, then shut
                down. You, met after that disaligning,
for years take your time. Ease
        entrance. Press, breathe, press.
                This is for you and your two fingers,
slender index, long middle, slightbent,
        testing pressure, testing give.
                And how, immediately after,
over and over, I still reverse
        too early to multi-valanced sleep,
                leaving you, stem and root, singly
unblossomed. You hum, *It's okay.*
        We have time. Take time. I take
                my breath, take my time, and try
to counter the spasm, the countless
        shutdown. For these moments
                I choose rare words: plateau,
catalectic, retrograde. From the ether
        a magazine hymns out the sacred
                directive: *Hetero Men: Deep Kiss,*
Use Your Fingers, Eat Puss.
        Every one of our windows
                boasts a stubborn square of sun
or not sun. Our cat clicks ill omen
        at the wire-walking robin. The thaws
                of the globe quicken. After my nerves
re-soften, after I open,
        you lie next to me, I sleep.
                This is for you and the swift

patience of your tongue,
        short-shrifted among my odes
                to lonely mothers, battered sunlight.
Your wild hair between me, the curve
        of your back as you give way
                in my hand. When my sleep
divides us with its creatured
        dreams, I mumble nonsense French,
                my throat shuts, over
and over, I gasp.
        You wake me. I consult doctors
                of sleeping, of breathing, and return home
to you, your hands, our waiting
        breath and, if I open then, we come at last
                to our equaling, our conduction.
For these moments, too, the rarest
        words: anemometer, percolation,
                zenith. Good thirst. Even in this world
an arc must still be possible.

Notes

The dedication to this book is an adaptation of Emily Dickinson's lines in "Except to Heaven, she is nought": "The smallest Housewife in the grass, / Yet take her from the Lawn / And somebody has lost the face / That made Existence – Home!"

The epigraph of **Waiting** is a direct quotation from Brenda Hillman's poem, "First Tractate," from her collection, *Death Tractates.*

In **Eclogue**, the line "It is vast and without sound" is an echo of Wallace Stevens's "Sunday Morning": "Winding across wide water, without sound. / The day is like wide water, without sound . . . "

Halfway through the Book I'm Writing is an imitation of Lynn Emanuel's poem of the same name from her book, *Then, Suddenly–*. It is a variation on the themes and structure of her poem, especially its conversation format and lines from its opening and closing stanzas: "Suddenly, I turn around and there he is" and "'Father,' I say, 'do you see them?' / And the phoebe says, Yes-squeak- / yes-squeak-yes-squeak-yes-squeak."

The opening lines of **Complicated Grief** are an adapted quotation of E. E. Cummings's poem, "my father moved through dooms of love."

In **Tending**, the word "syllableless" was coined by Emily Dickinson in her poem, "To tell the Beauty would decrease." The epigraph is a direct quotation from Vénus Khoury-Ghata's poem, "Orties" ("Nettles"), from the collection of the same name, translated by Marilyn Hacker.

The form of **Piccinini's "The Long Awaited"** is taken from Marianne Moore's "The Fish." The line, "The sea grows heavier in them," is adapted from her closing line, "The sea grows old in it." "The Long Awaited" refers to the sculpture of the same name by Patricia Piccinini.

Abduction is an imitation of Nuala Ní Dhomhnaill's poem, "Fuadach" ("Abduction"), translated by Michael Hartnett in *Selected Poems: Rogha Dánta,* and is a variation on the themes and motifs of her poem. The opening lines borrow from Ní Dhomhnaill's opening lines: "The fairy woman walked / into my poem. / She closed no door / She asked no by-your-leave." The imagery and syntax of the sixth and seventh stanzas draw from her lines, "For I am in the fairy field / in lasting darkness / and frozen with the cold there / dressed only in white mist."

The epigraph to **To the Supreme Associate Judges,** is from Medbh McGuckian's poem, "The Good Wife Taught Her Daughter," from her collection, *The Currach Requires No Harbours.* The phrase, "how little I must love / my windows," is adapted from her penultimate line, "So love your windows as little as you can."

The epigraph to **To the Next Supreme Justice,** is from the article, "The Return of the D.I.Y. Abortion," by Seth Stephens-Davidowitz, published in *The New York Times,* 5 March 2016.

After Tremor quotes the title of the article, "Hetero Men: Deep Kiss, Use Your Fingers, Eat Puss," by Aimée Lutkin, published in *Jezebel.com,* 24 February 2017.

Acknowledgments

My gratitude to the following journals in which these works first appeared, some of them in different versions:

The Adroit Journal: "What Mercy" (published as "Animal Cruelty")

The American Poetry Journal: "Piccinini's 'The Long Awaited'"

Barrow Street: "Complicated Grief"

Beloit Poetry Journal: "To the Supreme Associate Judges," and "You Have Two to Three Months, Maybe Less"

Best New Poets 2016: "Vigil Hemming In"

Crazyhorse: "After Arriving Home from Church and Learning Our Dogs Were Shot, Their Bodies in the Fields"

decomP magazinE: "Eclogue"

diode poetry journal: "Before the Diagnosis, Spring," "Exorcism Lessons in the Heartland," and "Now I'm a foregone conclusion, the voices in my head talk and talk . . ."

Great River Review: "Halfway through the Book I'm Writing," "Thorn Creek, Summer," and "Three Exposures"

Gulf Coast: "To the Next Supreme Justice,"

Harvard Review: "Hymeneal"

Indiana Review: "John Roberts,"

Iron Horse Literary Review: "Windfall" (published as "Resuscitating a Paralyzed Woman")

The Journal: "The Mound"

Permafrost: "Reservoirs"

Poetry Daily: "To the Next Supreme Justice," (reprinted)

Prelude Magazine: "Lying Old Together"

Salt Hill: "Weight"

The Southeast Review: "Resurrected, a version of my mother dwells in silence"

Southern Humanities Review: "Epode," "Tending," and "Vigil Hemming In" (reprinted)

Unsplendid: "After Waiting," "Tanka After-Hours," and "Waiting"

I am grateful to *Indiana Review* for choosing "Abduction" as a finalist for the 2016 *Indiana Review* Poetry Prize and for nominating "John Roberts," for a Pushcart Prize. I am also grateful to *Crazyhorse* for nominating "After Arriving Home from Church and Learning Our Dogs Were Shot, Their Bodies in the Fields" for inclusion in *Best New Poets 2019* and to the University of Arkansas for nominating "Before the Diagnosis, Spring" for the 2014 AWP: Intro Journals Project.

My immense thanks to Peter Covino, Sarah Kruse, Laura Marciano, and the entire editorial team at Barrow Street Press for their dedication to making this book a reality. Thank you, endlessly, to Ada Limón for choosing this book for the Barrow Street Book Prize.

Many thanks are owed to my teachers in the Creative Writing and English programs at Vanderbilt University, the University of Arkansas, and the University of Cincinnati for their inspiration and insight, especially Beth Bachmann, Geoffrey Brock, Kate Daniels, Geffrey Davis, John Drury, Rick Hilles, Mark Jarman, Rebecca Lindenberg, and Sandy Solomon.

I am indebted to my teachers at the University of Wisconsin-Madison, especially Quan Barry, Amaud Jamaul Johnson, and Ron Wallace, for ushering me into the world of poetry.

This book would not have been possible without those who offered their criticism throughout its drafts. Thank you, in particular, to Chad Abushanab, Christopher J. Adamson, Anthony Blake, Emily Rose Cole, Emily Cruz, Melissa Cundieff, Kimberly Grey, Zachary Harrod, Zachary Hester, J. Bailey Hutchinson, Yalie Kamara, Lisa Low, Michelle Myers, Sara Strong, Madeleine Wattenberg, Chelsea Whitton, Matthew Yeager, and Ricardo Zamorano Baez.

Thank you Feng Sun Chen, Lee Conell, Erika Geiser, Michelle Gibeault, Claire Jimenez, and D.J. Thielke for your wisdom, friendship, and encouragement.

To Katheryn Fronek, Dad, and Rachel, for your boundless bravery, strength, and support: thank you.

Patrick Rasico, thank you for believing in this book from the beginning and seeing it through to the end, for reading and rereading it in all its permutations, and for sharing your love and brilliance.

Kimberly Dees, there is no thanks enough for all you have done for this book and for me, but thank you all the same, for everything, always.

About the Author

Cara Dees has taught at the University of Cincinnati, Fisk University, Vanderbilt University, and the University of Arkansas. The recipient of a scholarship from the Sewanee Writers' Conference and an Academy of American Poets College Prize from the University of Wisconsin-Madison, her poetry has appeared in journals such as *Best New Poets, Gulf Coast, Harvard Review, Indiana Review, The Journal, Poetry Daily,* and *The Southeast Review.* Originally from rural Wisconsin, she holds an MFA from Vanderbilt University and is currently a PhD candidate at the University of Cincinnati.

Photo: Patrick Rasico

BARROW STREET POETRY

Exorcism Lessons in the Heartland
Cara Dees (2019)

American Selfie
Curtis Bauer (2019)

Hold Sway
Sally Ball (2019)

Green Target
Tina Barr (2018)

Adorable Airport
Jacqueline Lyons (2018)

Luminous Debris: New & Selected Legerdemain
Timothy Liu (2018)

We Walk into the Sea: New and Selected Poems
Claudia Keelan (2018)

Whiskey, X-ray, Yankee
Dara-Lyn Shrager (2018)

For the Fire from the Straw
Heidi Lynn Nilsson (2017)

Alma Almanac
Sarah Ann Winn (2017)

A Dangling House
Maeve Kinkead (2017)

Noon until Night
Richard Hoffman (2017)

Kingdom Come Radio Show
Joni Wallace (2016)

In Which I Play the Run Away
Rochelle Hurt (2016)

The Dear Remote Nearness of You
Danielle Legros Georges (2016)

Detainee
Miguel Murphy (2016)

Our Emotions Get Carried Away Beyond Us
Danielle Cadena Deulen (2015)

Radioland
Lesley Wheeler (2015)

Tributary
Kevin McLellan (2015)

Horse Medicine
Doug Anderson (2015)

This Version of Earth
Soraya Shalforoosh (2014)

Unions
Alfred Corn (2014)

O, Heart
Claudia Keelan (2014)

Last Psalm at Sea Level
Meg Day (2014)

Vestigial
Page Hill Starzinger (2013)

You Have to Laugh: New + Selected Poems
Mairéad Byrne (2013)

Wreck Me
Sally Ball (2013)

Blight, Blight, Blight, Ray of Hope
Frank Montesonti (2012)

Self-evident
Scott Hightower (2012)

Emblem
Richard Hoffman (2011)

Mechanical Fireflies
Doug Ramspeck (2011)

Warranty in Zulu
Matthew Gavin Frank (2010)

Heterotopia
Lesley Wheeler (2010)

This Noisy Egg
Nicole Walker (2010)

Black Leapt In
Chris Forhan (2009)